MACHINES MADE SIMPLE

Wedges

Written by Kirsty Holmes

KidHaven PUBLISHING

Published in 2026 by
KidHaven Publishing, an Imprint of
Greenhaven Publishing, LLC
2544 Clinton St., Buffalo, NY 14224

Written by: Kirsty Holmes
Edited by: Elise Carraway
Designed by: Amelia Harris

All facts, statistics, web addresses, and URLs in this book were verified as valid and accurate at time of writing. No responsibility for any changes to external websites or references can be accepted by either the author or publisher.

Cataloging-in-Publication Data
Names: Holmes, Kirsty.
Title: Wedges / Kirsty Holmes.
Description: Buffalo, NY : KidHaven Publishing, 2026. | Series: Machines made simple | Includes glossary and index.
Identifiers: ISBN 9781534550810 (pbk.) | ISBN 9781534550827 (library bound) | ISBN 9781534550834 (ebook)
Subjects: LCSH: Wedges--Juvenile literature. | Simple machines--Juvenile literature.
Classification: LCC TJ1201.W44 H65 2026 | DDC 621.9'92--dc23

Manufactured in the United States of America

CPSIA compliance information: Batch #CSKH26
For further information contact Greenhaven Publishing LLC at 1-844-317-7404.

Please visit our website, www.greenhavenpublishing.com.
For a free color catalog of all our high-quality books, call toll free 1-844-317-7404 or fax 1-844-317-7405.

Find us on

Image Credits

All images are courtesy of Shutterstock.com, unless otherwise stated. Cover – Svetliy, Shutterstock-Pixelsquid, Mega Pixel, Honourr. Recurring images – Onica Alexandru Sergiu. 2–3 – P24_Design, Heavypong, Inna_Kandybka. 4–5 – Roman Samborskyi, Romberi. 6–7 – Kunlathida6242, msgrafixx. 8–9 – cynoclub, LeonidKos. 10–11 – Inna_Kandybka, Marinodenisenko, JoannaTkaczuk, Jason Busa, Tomy Handoyo, JeremyShow. 12–13 – libor.pal, ja-aljona. 14–15 – BlueRingMedia, Yegor Larin. 16–17 – KateV28, Aleksandar Malivuk. 18–19 – Lucamato, lovelypeace. 20–21 – Bermek, Irenestev. 22–23 – Andrey Burmakin, Mega Pixel, Wlad74, Soloviova Liudmyla.

Contents

WORDS THAT LOOK LIKE <u>THIS</u> CAN BE FOUND IN THE GLOSSARY ON PAGE 24.

Marvelous Machinery

We use machines to help us in our everyday lives. Machines can help us do jobs that we could not do on our own. Look around you—can you see any machines right now?

COMPUTERS ARE COMPLICATED MACHINES THAT DO COMPLICATED JOBS.

Not all machines are complicated like computers. Some machines are really simple and do simple jobs. Axes are machines. You might not be able to play games on them, but they do important jobs.

AXES CHOP WOOD. YOU COULD NOT DO THAT WITH JUST YOUR HANDS.

What Is a Machine?

Machines help us do jobs that would be difficult to do ourselves. These jobs can be simple or complicated. Cars get us to different places. Washing machines clean clothes. Even pencil sharpeners are machines.

SIMPLE MACHINES DO SIMPLE JOBS. COMPLICATED MACHINES DO COMPLICATED JOBS.

Simple machines use forces to get jobs done. Forces, such as pushes or pulls, affect objects. They can change an object's speed or direction.

What Is a Wedge?

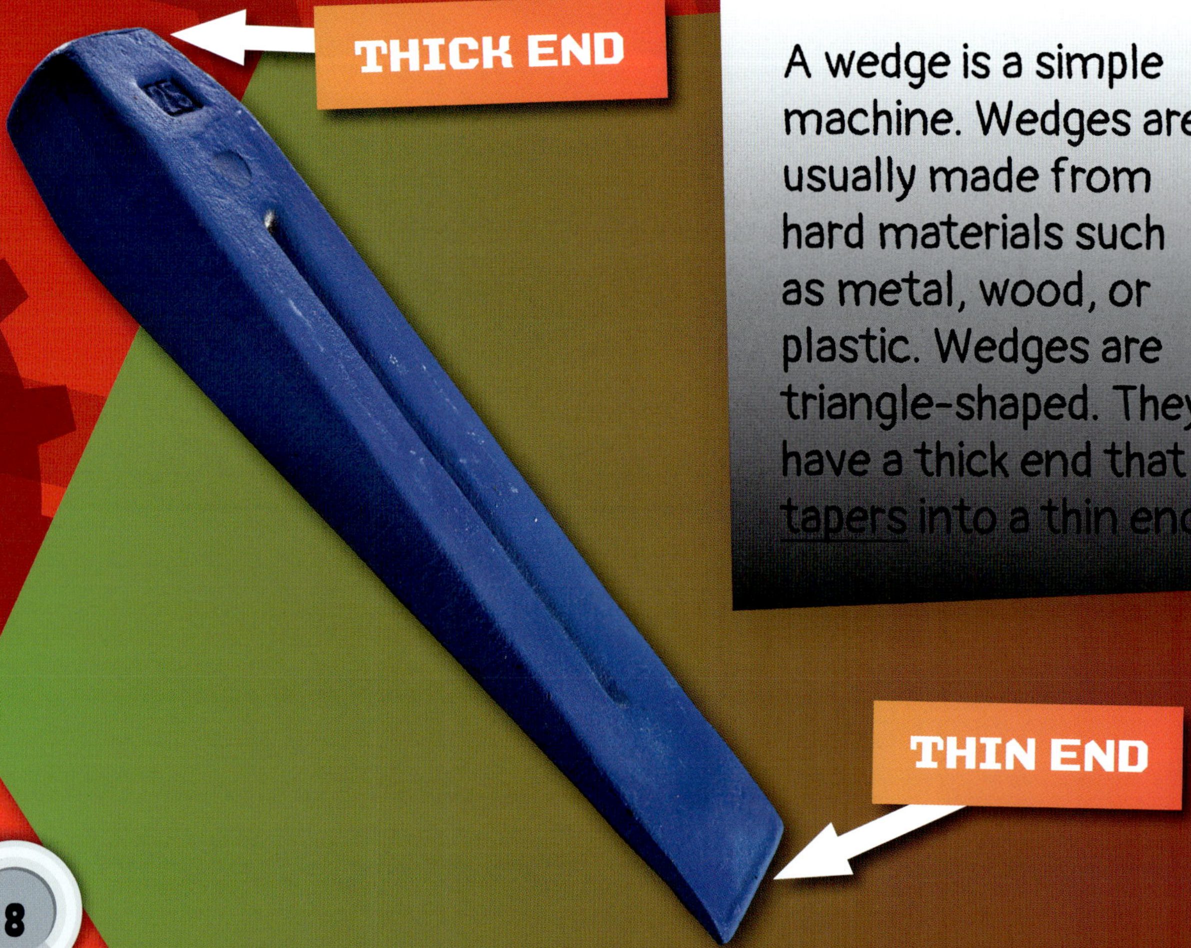

A wedge is a simple machine. Wedges are usually made from hard materials such as metal, wood, or plastic. Wedges are triangle-shaped. They have a thick end that tapers into a thin end.

A wedge uses the push from a person, known as input force, at the thick end, and turns it into a different kind of force at the thin end. This is called output force.

SHARP WEDGES CAN SPLIT MATERIAL, SUCH AS THIS WOOD.

Parts of a Wedge

All simple wedges have a thick end and a thin end. The sloping sides that join both ends together are called inclined planes. There are two main types of wedges—single wedges and double wedges.

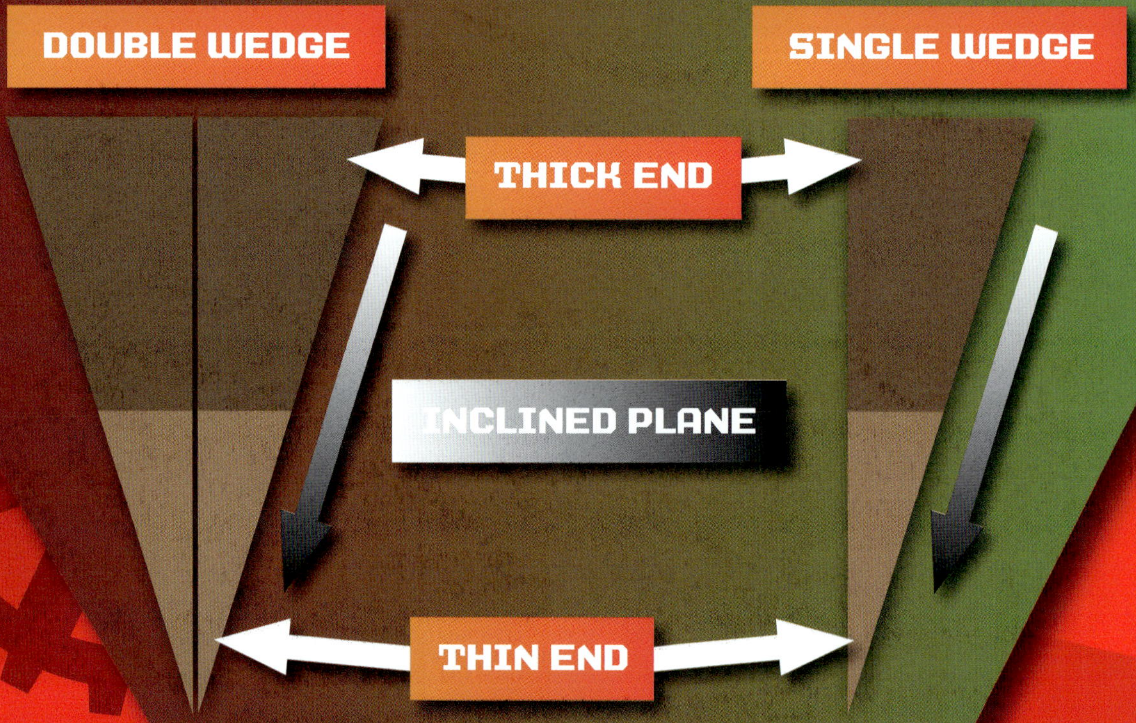

Wedges can be used for lots of things. They can...

Some wedges are used on their own. However, you can also use another tool, such as a hammer, to add more force.

Using hammers with splitting wedges helps lumberjacks split hard pieces of wood.

Other wedges have handles attached. This helps you put a bigger force on the wedge. The handle is usually at the thick end of the wedge.

An axe is a splitting wedge with a handle.

Working with Wedges

Wedges change the direction of the force you put in.

When a force pushes on the thick end, this pushes the thin end into the wood. The inclined planes push against the wood, changing its direction and pushing it apart.

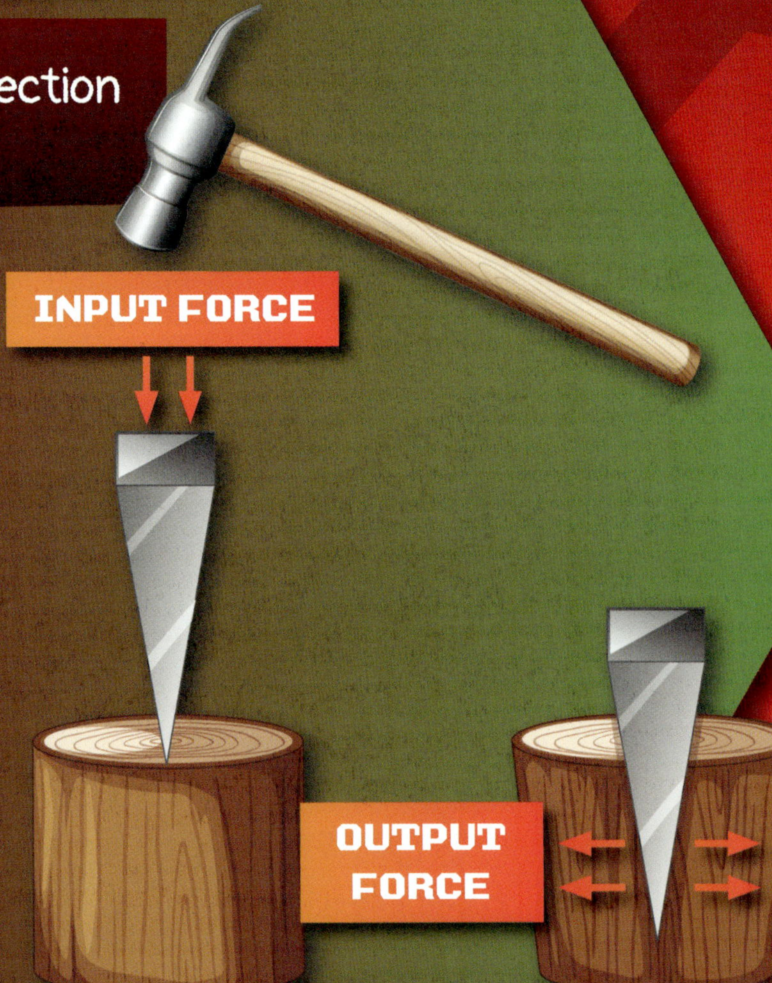

Long, thin wedges will be very sharp. This means they can do more work with less effort. If a wedge is shorter or has a wider tip, more effort is needed to do the same work.

CLEAVERS HAVE A LONG, THIN WEDGE ALONG THE EDGE. THEY CAN CUT THROUGH TOUGH MEATS.

Wedges for Splitting

Wedges can be used to split things apart. Splitting wedges need to be made from strong materials that can handle lots of force, such as metal. Splitting wedges can be hand tools or power tools.

THE INCLINED PLANES OF AN AXE ARE CALLED "CHEEKS."

Examples of Splitting Wedges

- Axes
- Spades
- Knives
- Front teeth
- Jackhammers

A jackhammer uses a motor to drive a wedge into a hard <u>surface</u>. The huge force splits the surface apart.

Wedges for Lifting

Wedges can be used for lifting things. If the wedge is pushed between the object and the surface, the object will be lifted up. The planes of the wedge separate the object from the surface.

WEDGE PLOWS CAN LIFT SNOW UP AND PUSH IT AWAY FROM RAILROAD TRACKS.

Examples of Lifting Wedges

- Plows
- Forklift forks
- Paint scrapers
- Spatulas

THE WEDGE SHAPE OF A SPATULA LETS YOU PUSH IT UNDER EGGS TO LIFT THEM UP.

Wedges for Stopping

Wedges can also hold things in place. People often use wedges to hold open doors. The thin end of the wedge fits under the door. The door gets stuck on the thick end and cannot move.

Examples of Holding Wedges

- Doorstops
- Wedge locks
- Nails and pins
- Chocks

Chocks are wedges that fit under wheels of large vehicles, such as trucks or airplanes. The wedges stop the wheels from rolling.

Super Simple

Wedges are one of the oldest simple machines. Ancient people used wedges as weapons and tools, such as spears, axes, and knives. These were often made of flint, a type of very hard rock.

Your teeth are wedges too! Your front teeth are called incisors. Incisors are wedge-shaped, with a thin cutting edge and a wider top. These are great for biting into foods.

Glossary

ancient	belonging to the very distant past
inclined planes	simple machines made up of a flat, tilted area
surface	the outside layer of something
tapers	gets narrower

Index